I WILL GET UP OFF OF

poetry by
SIMINA BANU

Coach House Books, Toronto

first edition

Canada Council   Conseil des Arts
for the Arts   du Canada   Canadä

ONTARIO ARTS COUNCIL
CONSEIL DES ARTS DE L'ONTARIO   Ontario
an Ontario government agency
un organisme du gouvernement de l'Ontario

Published with the generous assistance of the Canada Council for the
Arts and the Ontario Arts Council. Coach House Books also acknowl-
edges the support of the Government of Canada through the Canada
Book Fund and the Government of Ontario through the Ontario Book
Publishing Tax Credit.

LIBRARY AND ARCHIVES CANADA CATALOGUING IN PUBLICATION

Title: I will get up off of / Simina Banu.
Names: Banu, Simina, author.
Identifiers: Canadiana (print) 20240307453 | Canadiana (ebook)
2024030747X | ISBN 9781552454817 (softcover) | ISBN 9781770568112
(EPUB) | ISBN 9781770568129 (PDF)
Subjects: LCGFT: Poetry.
Classification: LCC PS8603.A62753 I29 2024 | DDC C811/.6—dc23

I Will Get Up Off Of is available as an ebook: ISBN 978 1 77056 811 2
(EPUB), 978 1 77056 812 9 (PDF)

Purchase of the print version of this book entitles you to a free digital
copy. To claim your ebook of this title, please email sales@chbooks.com
with proof of purchase. (Coach House Books reserves the right to
terminate the free digital download offer at any time.)

I will get up off of

this monobloc but I've been sentenced and now I am running through a field of memes. I tread softly, and they bite at my feet, relatably, godless. The memes are my companions, and I want to tell them how I've felt these days, because the memes will understand. They've been here too. They've felt like this, just like this. I know because they talk about their psychotherapists and their debts and their SSRIs and their exes and their microwaves and their possums. I trip. The memes encircle me, mouths agape like baby birds, and I feed them flesh from my eyes, and I feel loved.

this monobloc but look, a phone comes equipped with a calendar app, introducing the possibility of scrolling. A YouTuber exclaims each day is a jellybean, and lays 28,835 out onto the floor. I lose feeling in my thumb, and then the rest.

this monobloc but the cacophony of healthy people's meaning rattles up and down the hall. I don't think healthy people know their meaning looks like shit smeared around and around, all around. I don't think healthy people know their meaning is offensive, like a joke that doesn't land, or a hidden beet. I don't think healthy people know about luck, that I have a headache, my chakra blocked, dislodged and stretched over a melon.

this monobloc but I swallowed a story. It came up in my feed and I swallowed it, and now it is in me. It might be cake, and it might be a bag of money, but it can't be both. I wish the sun would stop. I wish these days worked. I wish I worked. And here I am, wished-out, like cake, like money.

this monobloc but the crystals I'm supposed to buy are across the province in a shop that closed before I was born. My vibration is so low that the neighbour keeps pounding on the wall, believing I am blasting music through multiple subwoofers. I assure him that it's just me and my low vibration. I explain that I cannot access the crystals I'm supposed to buy, so he should cut me some slack. I later find out that my vibrations have been unsettling his Pomeranian.

this monobloc but I've been so dehydrated ever since McNuggets began dropping from every faucet in my home. It goes like this: the pipes will gargle, because they are tortured, and the spout will exorcise nuggets, one by one, and they will flop into the sink: bone-like, ball-like, boot-like, bell-like.

this monobloc but the man explains that they do not sell coats here. He corrects himself because that's not entirely true. They have twenty or thirty coats, and he could sell me one, technically, but he thinks it wiser for me to talk to a coat specialist. I understand, but I have been really cold for months, years, I explain. I explain that friends are getting fed up with me. And look, I explain, a temperature specialist even confirmed, in writing, that I might be cold. The man understands, but it is wiser to see a coat specialist. In six months I will see a coat specialist, he explains. I explain that I can't wait that long, and the man nods, because he understands.

this monobloc but something hurts (an organ? a bone?), and therefore I shouldn't risk it.

this monobloc but Goya's dog drowned in mud. It's true the dog gazed upward, but she was looking at mud, and guess what, the mud wasn't looking at her. If we want to be accurate, she was looking at oil, she was oil, and everyone was plastered. Me too, over and over and over: the oil fills my stomach, and the mud fills me.

this monobloc but there is no monobloc. The monobloc creaks under no weight. I catch a glimpse of myself in the Zoom call, but there is no Zoom, only thousands of birds converging outside my window, zigzagging in and out of formation, ping-ponging on and off of no windows, witnessing nothing.

this monobloc but the tea worked, and the melatonin, and the weed. The beer worked too, until it stopped working, in solidarity, a little after I stopped working. The tongue stopped working, stopped saying stuff, and the nose stopped working too, but that might have been COVID. I don't remember when the eyes stopped working, but it was likely September, before the stomach stopped working, but after the lungs.

this monobloc but the man tells me to practise something. The man tells me to practise breathing in a T-shirt. I do it every morning, but I have my doubts. The man explains that it will help me locate the pain so that I can notice it and let it go. I explain that someone is taking a hammer to my foot. I know what is happening, I explain, someone is bashing my foot with a hammer. While this exercise might help a person who feels pain and has trouble finding hammers, I am able to draw a diagram that clearly points to my hammer, and even to the asshole who's wielding it: me. The man empathizes, but he explains that I really should meditate, because how else will I find the hammer? I explain to the man that I no longer care about the hammer and just want my toes to stop bleeding. The man waves his hands understandingly and directs me to the App Store. This app is 65 percent off. Wouldn't I love to receive detailed infographics about all the different types of hammers, as well as personalized guidance on how to find them?

this monobloc but Pabst, Mill Street, Mill Street, Guinness, Sapporo, Mill Street, Boréale, Boréale, Mill Street, Boréale, Miller, Pabst, Okanagan, Blue Moon, Mill Street, Blue Moon, Blue Moon, Blue Moon, Blue Moon, Blue Moon, Blue Moon, Sapporo, Pabst, Boréale, Boréale, Pabst, Okanagan, Corona, Heineken (yuck), Heineken, Boréale, Boréale, Boréale, Boréale, Boréale, Boréale, Mill Street, Mill Street, Mill Street, La Fin Du Monde, Mill Street, La Fin Du Monde,

this monobloc but I can't seem to manifest movement, despite listening to podcasts.

this monobloc but it is so complicated with so many muscles involved. There are the quadriceps and hamstrings doing the heavy lifting, and gastrocnemius muscles, which straighten the body as it rises. But it is also important to engage the obliques, glutes, and rectus abdominis to avoid overworking the legs. If I had a spine, the erector spinae would also be involved, and certainly the gluteus maximus, gluteus medius, and gluteus minimus, or more colloquially, the gluteus venti, gluteus grande, and gluteus tall. I could use the biceps and triceps for extra assistance, and maybe combine them with the deltoids and latissimus dorsi, but hopefully it doesn't come to that. There is also the issue of monobloc height. The lower the seat, the more activated each muscle group needs to be to provide lift. Unfortunately, it is difficult to assess the appropriate level of activation while I am on the monobloc itself, and with so many steps, it is also difficult to remember the order. If the sequence is incorrect, I may fail to balance and stabilize, and I risk falling even lower than I already am.

this monobloc but I can't fucking draw it.

this monobloc but now is a good time for some history. While the first instance of monobloc ('one' + 'block') is unknown, earliest accounts date back to second millennium BCE Mesopotamia, where the matter was delegated to priests, and often required exorcism. Many scholars believe that monoblocs have been around for the whole span of human history, and likely developed due to a hyperactive amygdala. However, the first modern instance of a monobloc came in 1972, when Henry Massonnet designed his Fauteuil 300. Unpatented, it spread quickly into all corners of the world, a phenomenon experts attribute to the monobloc's unique propensity to stack.

this monobloc but I can't get a grip on any of these Quora answers. I slip off one and onto another and then off that one too. I need a Quora answer to tell me I'm okay, that I'm not as dying or dead as I think I am, but instead each one grabs me by the collar and whispers something demonic before finally devouring my thumb.

this monobloc but this poem isn't here. You can find this poem is on page_25.

this monobloc but some people wear suits. Where do they find a suit? Some people are walking around wearing suits on the subway, and if they're not walking, they're standing, only because it's too crowded to walk, but suited people know standing is a temporary disorder, and soon they're walking again, all duded up, and they walk confidently, in lines, in suits, and even though there are so many lines, cutting into one another, colliding, they know exactly which one is theirs, and they order a grande, because suited people are moderate, picking up a work call, a child, emailing a dentist, suiting.

this monobloc but where would I go? a beanbag? a sofa? a stool? a folding chair? Surely not a chaise longue. A bench? a stump? a recliner? an overturned bucket? an executive chair? a car seat? the floor? the grass? a fence? a ledge?

this monobloc but La Fin Du Monde, La Fin
Du Monde, Mill Street, Maudite, La Fin Du
Monde, Maudite, Maudite, Diet Coke, Pepsi,
Pepsi, LaCroix, Coors, Coors, Maudite, Blue
Moon, Brahma, Brahma, Mini Meister from my
pocket, Brahma, Coors, LaCroix, LaCroix,
LaCroix, La Fin Du Monde, Mini Meister from
my pocket, Mini Meister from my pocket, Mill
Street, Brahma, Mini Meister from my pocket,
Mill Street, Heineken (yuck), Heineken (yuck),
Heineken (yuck), Heineken, Heineken, La Fin
Du Monde, La Find Du Monde, Grey Goose,
Heineken, LaCroix, Pepsi,

this monobloc but the hazelnut cake fell in the middle of the No Frills, and it got all smeared on the newly renovated floor. Everyone watched as I picked it up and pressed it to my chest. I thought about hiding it behind the Pop Tarts but no, I understood the cake was mine now. I considered dropping one of us in the trash, but it was overflowing with masks. Anyway, it was too late. I scraped off the frosting that had been in contact with the newly renovated floor, gently, surgically, and I sanitized the remaining cake, sprayed it down with Lysol, and I stared at it until it rotted.

this monobloc but I only captured 226 of the 48,298 spiders who arrived today.

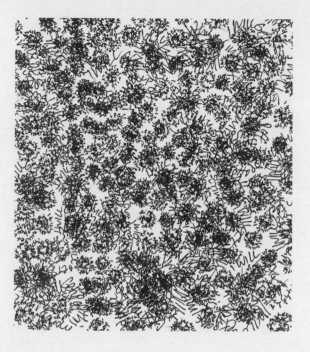

this monobloc but eye floaters, everywhere I turn.

this monobloc but 226 thoughts, of 48,298
negative thoughts, of a total 62,997 thoughts:
imagine trying to see through that. I have carpel
tunnel from the Whac-A-Mole. Wednesday is
nothing, again.

this monobloc but it is uncommon to release sentences from down here. There are few opportunities for sentences in the first place because people stop dropping by to catch them. When sentences aren't set loose, neither are any thoughts and feelings, since thoughts and feelings need an escort. After a long period of silence, when a sentence is finally preparing to exit through an open mouth, escorting a chill thought about hockey or *Love Island*, the thoughts and feelings who have been most distressed by confinement jump onto the sentence's shoulders and hold tight to its arms and legs. Sentences are sensitive and want to accommodate everyone, so now I've got one sentence escorting four thoughts and six feelings. The real problem is in exiting the mouth. If a sentence can't fit, it either gives up or else tries to force itself through, breaking up the thoughts and feelings into jagged, sharp fragments, which risk injuring the person who has shown up to catch them.

this CHAIR

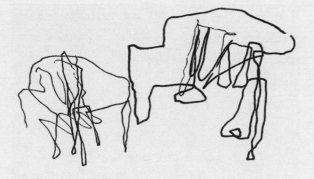

this monobloc but I fear I am becoming experimental with my attempts. Last night I tried to hoist myself up by gripping onto bananas taped all over the walls. They couldn't bear the weight of something: me? Sometimes the tape would peel the paint right off the wall, revealing a horrifying yellow undercoat, and other times the banana would just split, leaving me banana-handed but utterly seated.

this monobloc but must I get up off the monobloc? Really? I could just cover the monobloc with a bedsheet. No one would be able to spot it then, unless it goes *boo*, or I get tangled up in it. Then I can carry it around town and we can get up to all sorts of trouble. The only problem is weight. The weights of monoblocs aren't standardized at production: they're custom-made each time. So my ex Chelsea's monobloc might be lighter than my pal Will's, but they both might be heavier than frenemy Katie's. It's impossible to know since we have only one word for it. I do know I can't seem to carry it too far, especially with the sheet on it, so I'll have to re-evaluate the strategy tomorrow.

this monobloc but this poem isn't here. You can find this poem on page_37.

this monobloc but this poem isn't here. You can
find this poem on page_38.

this monobloc but my psychic is just about ready to give up on me. First I couldn't find the crystals I was supposed to buy, then I fidgeted too much in the reiki session, now I spilled Pepsi on all the tarot cards. She says I'm sabotaging myself. She says I've given up. 'Look around,' she says, tenderly fanning Death, 'everyone is trying to help you. Everyone! You take a tiny sip of Help, wrinkle your nose, and announce it doesn't work. It tastes bad. You've given it your best shot but it's just not good enough. So off you go in search of a perfect potion, or a perfect saviour, or at least a perfect escape. You say you don't believe in woo – the truth is you don't believe in anything. You don't believe in life.'

this monobloc but gravity has been heavier than usual these past few weeks, so as a precaution I grab the nearest marker and scribble NOT CAKE all over my body.

this monobloc but Pepsi, Pepsi, LaCroix, Pepsi, Diet Coke, Coke, Coke Zero, Coke, Pepsi, Pepsi, Pepsi, LaCroix, Pepsi, Perrier, Perrier, Pepsi, Perrier, LaCroix (yuck), LaCroix (yuck), LaCroix (yuck), LaCroix (yuck), LaCroix (yuck), Pepsi, LaCroix (yuck), LaCroix (yuck), Pepsi, Pepsi, Sprite, Sprite, LaCroix (yuck), LaCroix (I shake my fist at the ceiling. Universe! Can't you see I'm trying?),

this monobloc but the podcast episode with the surprise poem about grief was touching: it travelled through my body like guided meditation – I noticed a couplet in my chest as it infiltrated my shoulder and then rushed down my forearm into my fingertips, and it hurt, sure – couplets in arteries will cause all sorts of trouble: coronary vandalism, irreparable damage – but at least gravity retreated. I could feel my hands again, I could feel my legs, and then, without warning, a final surprise: it blossomed from the closing words of the poem, which at this point were radiating from all my limbs, and it spoke so much louder than anything that had come before, climbing to the ceiling and bouncing into all the corners, frightening the spiders, frightening me. The word from our sponsors rushed through my body like detergent, and before I knew it, everything was gone again.

this monobloc but I can't decide who to trust. @awakenwithkris just offered to spray the monobloc every morning with personalized affirmations. She says that in time the spray will corrode the monobloc's legs and one day they'll just break. I try to get clarification on where my body will land in that case: Will I just be sitting on the floor on the shards of my former monobloc? Will it hurt? She doesn't reply but instead links me to her monthly affirmations package, which is 65 percent off, but only for the next 59 minutes. I am about to click Buy when @lionpowermindset catapults into my feed, headbutting @awakenwithkris off-screen. Am I sick of self-help gurus selling me useless, cookie-cutter BS that ultimately leaves me feeling like shit? Am I sick of generic statements like 'love yourself' that are completely lacking in insight on how to actually get better? @lionpowermindset's zero-bullshit approach to self-improvement will get me off my ass and moving toward my goals. He offers real, gritty solutions I don't want to hear. I'll be off that monobloc in no time with his personalized extreme action plan, 65 percent off for a limited time – I want to know more, but @lionpowermindset's pitch is cut short by what appear to be thousands of minimalist bottles flying in his direction. They pummel him, forming a small hill. I swipe down to see @balance.aroma.s ascend from the luminous pile. Have I heard of bergamot? This lesser-known essential oil will change my life.

TM

this monobloc but I worry I'm alone. #BellLets-
Talk keeps telling me to talk, that the first step
is the hardest, but I'm not so sure. Bell insists: it
understands, everyone understands. Okay, what
if I do say how I feel. What if I say I feel like
this*:

*this is not how I actually feel, just an example

and it turns out everyone else has been feeling
like this:

or worse! – maybe everyone else, this whole time, has been feeling like this:

Then I'll really be a freak. 'Get a load of that feeling!' someone will yell upon discovering my feeling. A small group of concerned citizens will form, encircling the feeling, whispering to one another, pointing: 'Look at the curvature of that thing!' a woman will say, appalled, peeking between her fingers. 'And that pointy bit? Yikes. Nothing to be done but let nature run its course,' a coat specialist will say, adjusting his glasses. 'Hopefully it's put out of its misery soon enough,' a man will say as he pulls his dachshund's rain hood over its eyes.

– wait, I got off. Because the monobloc is on fire. Something ignited it and instead of melting it just shot up in flames. I ran off of it and tried to sit on the couch, but instantly that lit up too. So then I tried sitting on the hardwood and now the whole apartment is ablaze. I'm worried the problem might be me. Desperate, I turn on the faucet – it spits out McNuggets. They're spilling out of the sink onto the floor, where they instantly explode into ash. It's a horrible sight. I feel something in my chest, something hiccupping, so I grab my phone to try to tweet for help, but my hands are trembling. To make matters worse, now the goddamn neighbour's Pomeranian is barking. I remember I didn't double-check my bike lock, and I remember that thing I said to Sara, who surely was hurt, and that thing I didn't say to Jeff, and I remember that time I was in the hospital, because my arm wasn't cake, and that other time, and that other time. Now I can't stop remembering, and I definitely didn't lock the bike, and I don't have enough money for rent next month. Worst of all, I remember I love all these people, really love them, and I'll never reach them again because I can't, because now McNugget ash is up to my elbows, I can't move, and that dog –

I think I'm gonna shut it all down.
Yeah, I'm gonna shut it all down.

this monobloc but maybe it's not so bad down here. This monobloc can really be quite comfortable. If I sit perfectly still nothing will find me.

this monobloc but I thought this Zoom was with a coat specialist. It's been four months. This Zoom is with a temperature coordinator. She wants to assess how cold I've been, broadly, to determine whether I'm at risk of freezing to death. If I'm about to freeze to death, I need to call a hotline. She's given me a bunch of numbers. Unfortunately, I'm not in the correct coat jurisdiction. I need to exit one coat jurisdiction and enter another in order to access a coat specialist. It's a lot of paperwork, likely another four months, but in the meantime there is an app.

this monobloc but this poem isn't here. You can find this poem on page_55.

this monobloc but this poem isn't here. You can find this poem on page_56.

this monobloc but I may be a real asshole. I'm freezing to death on page_25 as the comments roll in. I resent page_25, that it helps people. People are reading page_25 and hopping off their monoblocs and drinking a smoothie, and I'm freezing to death on page_25. I don't understand – do I have monobloc premium? I wouldn't be surprised. I always sign up for the free trial and forget to cancel.

this monobloc but nothing did find me, and
now it's vacuuming up all my nuggets, all my
ash, and me. Soon this room will be quite clean.

this monobloc, which is right at the core of something: me. The me is surrounded by millions of little monobloc particles, like

 , , and .

The particles push into me. Some of them are sharp, and they cut when they enter my consciousness, and some have rounder edges that press hard, causing a constant ache.

I do not let the particles exit so they don't worry anyone – or, worse, confuse them, confirming my aloneness. So when choosing anything to say, I make sure to choose from the layer of sayable things that is farthest away from the me. That way I don't risk any monobloc particles hitching a ride:

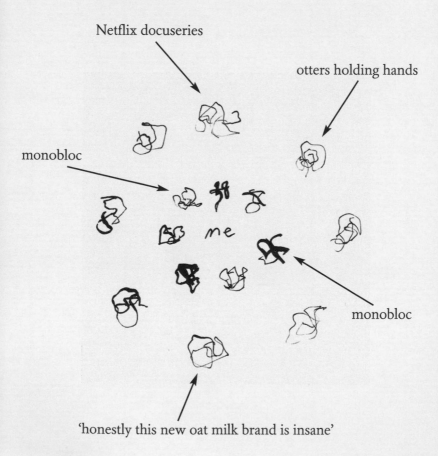

Netflix docuseries

otters holding hands

monobloc

me

monobloc

'honestly this new oat milk brand is insane'

With time, however, I stop being able to express anything in direct vicinity of the me. The monobloc stays hidden, and so do other things, making the strategy far from ideal:

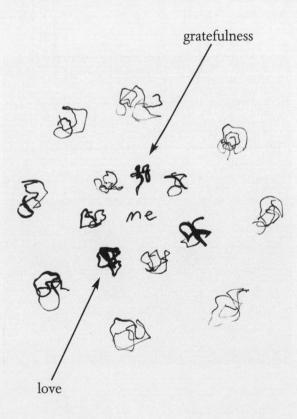

this monobloc but the monobloc has been shar-
pening its edges. The armrests, in particular, are
a safety hazard. I file the edges down sometimes
with random tools I've collected over the years.
Sometimes a song or some CBT can do the trick,
but increasingly, I have to sleep or cry for days
before the surface is smooth enough to safely
rest on. I'm losing. It doesn't help that monoblocs
are eloquent speakers – convincing rhetoricians
– and fucking word thieves. It is not uncommon
for a monobloc to give orders, instructing its
host to repeat after it. My monobloc tells me I
don't want to live, and after months of resisting,
I say it back – to try it out, to see how it feels.
But the problem is that a monobloc will save
those words, record them. So the next time it
tells me I don't want to live, my own voice echoes
along with it, like a malfunctioning Zoom call.
And every subsequent instance I say it back is
added to the demon choir. This is how the
monobloc sharpens itself. This is how I end up
on Google, with hundreds of pages of bridges.

this? but sometimes the only thing keeping the speaker of this poem from googling a bridge a little too determinedly is emails: all the emails she would have to send. To imagine typing out those emails is enough to drain the speaker of all the energy required to google bridges.

this. The poem isn't here. You can find this poem on page_64.

this. Don Marquis's moth keeps visiting me in
the middle of the night and giving what I can
only assume are pep talks:

good evening i am the moth
from your favourite poem
in high school
i fried myself a long
long time ago
still
you may think
i was never on a monobloc
because moths dont do that
but because i am a poem
i know a thing or two
about monoblocs
on a molecular level

you see when you are so
so low
you create extra art molecules
it s just something that happens
but because art is necessarily
a hopeful undertaking
it needs to attach to a hope molecule
to exit your body as art
even the darkest grimiest art molecule
needs a hope molecule
to activate

unfortunately the monobloc pins all the hope
in a secret corner of your body
who knows where
an earlobe
a toe
somewhere the art wont think
to look

thats the problem
bodies will always generate hope
but locating it
with that tyrant around
is no joke

the good news is
if even one art molecule
can find the secret stash
it might let loose
the rest

art molecules are like bees
in that they have a complex dance
to direct the hive
to where it needs to be

anyway
i ll only ask you one more time
do you have a lighter

this

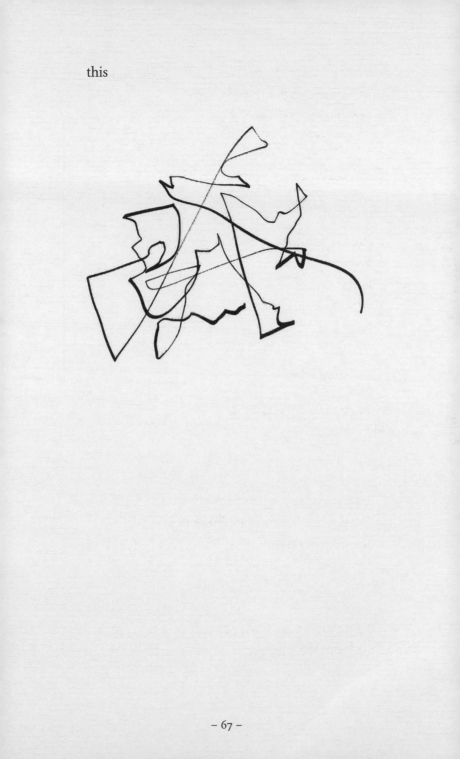

ACKNOWLEDGEMENTS

So much gratitude to the Coach House team for believing in *I Will Get Up Off Of* and bringing it to life – thank you for taking a chance on the weirdness of this book. Thanks especially to Crystal Sikma, for the gorgeous design, James Lindsay, for helping the book reach people, and Alana Wilcox, for perfecting the last details.

Forever grateful to my genius editor, Susan Holbrook. Not only is the book better because of you, but I wouldn't be writing poetry at all if not for your guidance and support over the years. Thank you.

Enormous thanks to my friends who provided feedback on versions of this manuscript: Amilcar John Nogueira, Gwen Aube, Lee Reid, Fan E, Dan McAndrew, and Mark Coldham. Your friendship and support means the world to me.

Very grateful to Gerardo Salazar for all of the photos.

Thank you to my parents for always being there for me.

This manuscript was written with support from the Canada Council for the Arts.

Simina Banu is a writer and musician living in Montreal. She likes investigating the inexpressibility of feelings, of anxiety and depression against the backdrop of capitalism, technology, and the Internet. *I Will Get Up Off Of* is her second book. She has also written *POP* (Coach House Books, 2020) and several chapbooks.

Typeset in Aragon and Adobe Handwriting Ernie.

Printed at the Coach House on bpNichol Lane in Toronto, Ontario, on Zephyr Antique Laid paper, which was manufactured, acid-free, in Saint-Jérôme, Quebec, from second-growth forests. This book was printed with vegetable-based ink on a 1973 Heidelberg KORD offset litho press. Its pages were folded on a Baumfolder, gathered by hand, bound on a Sulby Auto-Minabinda, and trimmed on a Polar single-knife cutter.

Coach House is located in Toronto, which is on the traditional territory of many nations, including the Mississaugas of the Credit, the Anishnabeg, the Chippewa, the Haudenosaunee, and the Wendat peoples, and is now home to many diverse First Nations, Inuit, and Métis peoples. We acknowledge that Toronto is covered by Treaty 13 with the Mississaugas of the Credit. We are grateful to live and work on this land.

Edited by Susan Holbrook
Cover and interior design by Crystal Sikma, cover art *Monobloc Plastic Chair* by Rosi Feist
Author photo by Gerardo Salazar

Coach House Books
80 bpNichol Lane
Toronto ON M5S 3J4
Canada

mail@chbooks.com
www.chbooks.com